Disclaimer

No part of this publication is intended to diagnose, treat, or cure any illness. Nothing contained within these pages is to be construed as medical advice.

The author accepts no responsibility or liability for the application of any of the methods, commands or exercises described in this publication.

For entertainment and information purposes only.

Please dowse responsibly and only with other's permission if dowsing on behalf of someone else.

Please follow the safety protocols in this book before dowsing on behalf of another. By buying this book and using pendulum healing on another you are declaring that you know about and understand how to dowse safely for another person and are an experienced dowser.

Copyright

Contents

Contents

*The grid above is an energy
amplification grid. You
can direct energy with it
using the pendulum clockwise
to amplify your pendulum
commands by the power of 10.
Surrounded by gold which is great
for manifesting and healing.*

KEY POINTS TO *Remember*

We are all connected
All healing is self-healing
You create your own reality
Your beliefs shape your reality
You can make friends with time
Everything is made of energy
You can easily change your timeline
You are more powerful than you can dream of
You can change your past, present, and future
You have a team of helpers in a higher dimension
Your body is aware of your thoughts and feelings
You can connect to any energy in the universe
You are more than your physical body
You can undo or reverse any command
Everything happens in the now
Life is an adventure and the
universe is your playground

It's time to remember
how magical you are

What is a pendulum?

The pendulum is a fast effective metaphysical tool for connecting with your inner guidance system or the elements, frequencies and vibration of the universe.

It can be used for internal and external transformation, empowerment, spiritual development and energy healing. It is thought that over the next few years energy medicine will become increasingly more well known as the old ways of working with energy are replaced with higher frequency based modalities that utilise light and sound.

Why use a pendulum for dowsing?

Knowledge and information is empowering and it is said that all the information you seek is already within, using a pendulum is a direct way to access these inner secrets by connecting to your higher self for divine guidance. Sounds magical, doesn't it.

Using 0 - 100% or dowsing charts you can discover what is most beneficial for you or your cat at any time whether it's food, supplements, colour, modalities...even people.

Basically, anything under the sun!

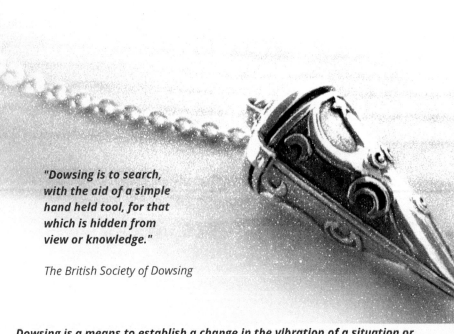

> *"Dowsing is to search,
> with the aid of a simple
> hand held tool, for that
> which is hidden from
> view or knowledge."*

The British Society of Dowsing

Dowsing is a means to establish a change in the vibration of a situation or event or of an animal, person or object by tuning into, accessing and changing the wave patterns that exist in the universe as energy fields of intelligent information. Also known as subtle energy fields.

Using the pendulum to dowse takes the guesswork out of psychic awareness and as you develop your dowsing you are likely to also develop your clairvoyance skills as you tune into higher frequencies and brain wave patterns.

Dowsing and pendulum healing offers unlimited choices and options for:

- *Correcting energy imbalances*
- *Increasing ability to make better choices from inner wisdom*
- *Increasing awareness of energy and self mastery*
- *Clearing old emotions, habits and subconscious energy patterns*
- *Direct cellular communication for energy healing*
- *Reprogramming the subconscoius mind for positive outcomes*
- *Going back in time and changing the energy of an event to influence the future*
- *Sending healing to your cat much like Reiki does*
- *Repairing the relationship between you and your cat*
- *Water imprinting Bach remedies for cellular emotional healing*
- *Testing food/objects/ideas for strengthening or weakening frequencies*

Using the pendulum for the first time

You first need to tune into the pendulum and see how it moves for you and your energy system. This is the first step in programming a pendulum.

A pendulum's movements

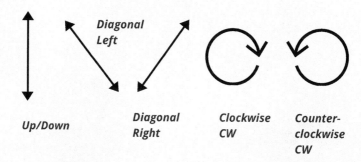

Up/Down

Diagonal Left

Diagonal Right

Clockwise CW

Counter-clockwise CW

You can direct it by speaking to it and asking questions or commands either out loud or in your mind. Both work effectively.

1. Feet on the floor sitting comfortably with arm by your side and not resting on a table.

2. Hold the pendulum a few inches from the base between thumb and index finger.

3. Ask the pendulum, "Show me the movement for YES." Note it and right it down. "Show me the movement for NO." Note it and write it down.

YES _____

NO _____

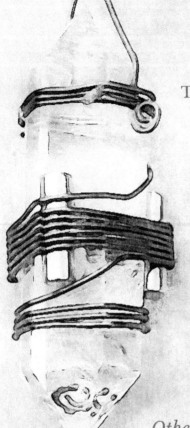

THE PENDULUM WILL EITHER MOVE IN STRAIGHT LINES, HORIZONTALLY OR IN CIRCULAR MOVEMENTS

Make a note of the direction your pendulum moves in the spaces provided for yes, no. My yes is up and down and my no is side to side but that is just for some of my pendulums, each may respond differently.

The pendulum can also move direction where yes is clockwise and no is counterclockwise. If your pendulum does not move at all then decide which way you would like it to move for yes and move it in that way stating this is my yes, then repeat this with a different movement for no and don't know.

Other ways to work with YES/NO

When I need quick answers from the pendulum I just write YES and NO on a piece of paper and then just ask the question out loud and the pendulum will answer by showing me either Yes or No as it swings to one of the words. For me this is the quickest way, grab a pen and paper and away you go.

Ask some questions that you know the answer to for yes and no and see how the pendulum responds, you will gravitate to one way of working and use that.

Some people find it easier to just use dowsing charts to measure energy. The most common is the 0 - 100% chart where you can measure any energy as a scale by simply asking, "Everything in the universe considered what is the percentage of _____?"

Pre-session dowsing protocol

Polarity

Your energy body is electric and magnetic, these energy circuits can become disrupted causing an imbalance, this is called reversed polarity and will affect your dowsing. Tapping the side of your hand re-balances this.

Hydration

If your physical body is hydrated then energy and information runs through your system easier than if you are dehydrated. Pure water will clear your chakras, meridians and even non-beneficial energy so take a glass of water before your session

Clearing the Astral

It is important you measure how much non-beneficial energy from the astral is affecting the session before you begin. Use a 0 - 100% chart and ask, "What % of non-beneficial energy is affecting this healing session now?" A clearing command is below:

 "I release all negative energy from my space, auric field and this healing session now. All energy released is transformed into love and sent to the Central Sun for clearing, I only allow divine love and highest vibrational energy to be present."

Increasing accuracy rate

You can increase your accuracy rate simply by requesting it with a command such as this one:

 "Increase accuracy rate of my pendulum dowsing and healing for this and all sessions. All interference is null and void, the pendulums only listens to the sound of my voice and takes instruction from my commands."

You can also ask to activate Spiritual Law which is the right to explore the universe without interference. Dowse and see how effective this concept is as a protection method. Grounding, protection and connection will be discussed in more detail next.

Pendulum Commands

Pendulum commands are spoken statements that connect with the frequency of the pendulum with your intention to change the probability of something happening in your favour. The pendulum is a tool for accessing information at the subtle realms usually not available to connec to.

Before you pick up the pendulum decide what you want to ask or know or do. Think about what you want to achieve.

Removing or clearing is done commanding a sentence in your mind or speaking it out loud whilst spinning the pendulum counterclockwise. When the pendulum has finished spinning your command is finished and the energy around this issue you are dowsing for will have changed.

A CCW example of a pendulum clearing command:

"Remove all non-beneficial energy affecting my auric energy field and subtle energy body now for my highest good and the highest good of all concerned."

Pendulum Clearing Words:

- **Release**
- **Eliminate**
- **Clear to zero**
- **Scramble**
- **Dissolve**
- **Disable**
- **Disconnect**
- **Eradicate**
- **Disintegrate**
- **Collapse timeline of**

Counterclockwise is used with a clearing, removing or disconnecting command when you want to remove something from your timeline, subtle energy body or energy memory.

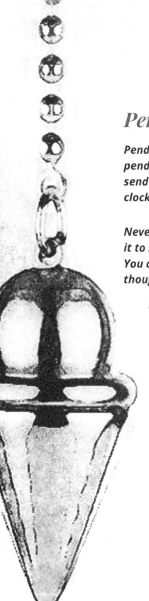

Pendulum installing words

Pendulum installing commands are done with a clockwise pendulum spin. With these installing words you are looking to send in new energy with the pendulum. Use these words with a clockwise movement to shift energy forwards or bring in the new.

Never interrupt the pendulum whilst it is spinning, wait for it to stop before starting with the next command.
You can program a list of commands to all run at the same time though.

Installing energy is a clockwise command such as:

"Raise my vibration to one of love" or "Activate my heart chakra with love for my highest good and the highest good of all concerned."

Installing Words:

- Expand
- Send in
- Enhance
- Empower
- Accelerate
- Energise
- Deliver
- Power up
- Activate

- Improve
- Assist
- Allow
- install
- Run program of
- Integrate
- Embrace
- Transform
- Turbo-charge

Clockwise pendulum movement is used for installing, imprinting, activating or allowing commands when you want to action new energy or increase energy.

Working with energy

Every possibility and potential outcome for our
future exists in the now moment.
We are vortexes of light transmitting and
receiving energy and the pendulum
is just an extension of this and a tool that directs energy as
a living consciousness.

An atom is 99.9% invisible space, if you took out the space
in our atoms the whole of the human population would fit
into a sugar cube.

Some call it The Field, some have made orgonite with it,
others call it Chi or Prana and use it to clear energetic
blockages in the body.

The Law of Attraction manages this energy
with your inner vibration or frequency. We can use the
pendulum to raise the vibration of our energy or
consciousness by asking to

Vibrational frequency for manifesting chart

A vibrational scale such as this one will empower you to vibrate higher than your current level for faster manifesting. You can use it daily to check the level you are currently vibrating at and then using a clockwise pendulum spin to raise the level of vibration.

The higher the level of vibration the easier it is to manifest!

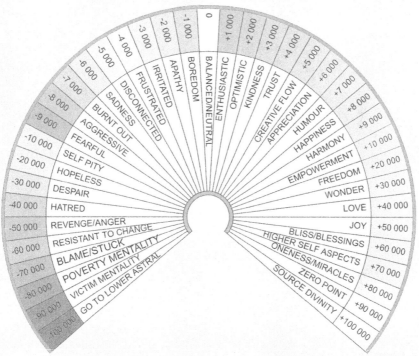

Check the vibration of food/water or any part of the body for manifesting.

A clockwise pendulum spin will raise the vibration of anything you wish to by asking to do it. Wait for the pendulum to stop and then dowse the vibration rate after the healing has been done.

Ask the cells in the body to access joy then dowse test it.

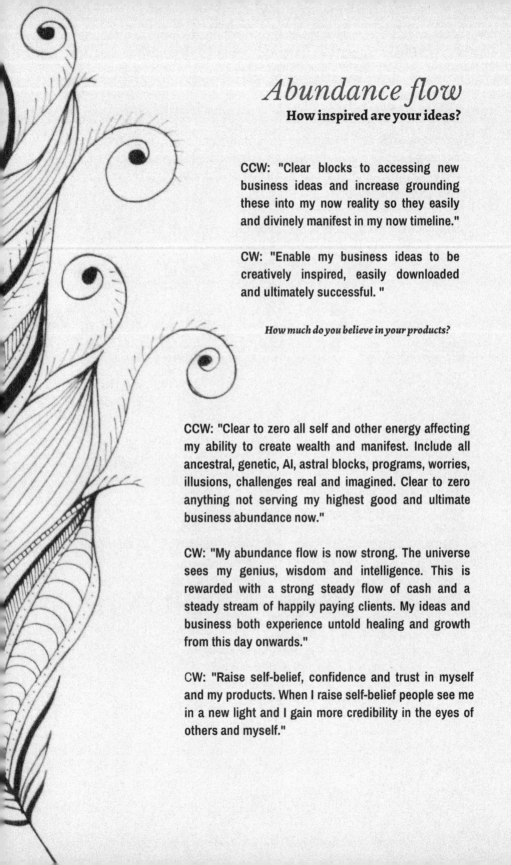

Abundance flow

How inspired are your ideas?

CCW: "Clear blocks to accessing new business ideas and increase grounding these into my now reality so they easily and divinely manifest in my now timeline."

CW: "Enable my business ideas to be creatively inspired, easily downloaded and ultimately successful. "

How much do you believe in your products?

CCW: "Clear to zero all self and other energy affecting my ability to create wealth and manifest. Include all ancestral, genetic, AI, astral blocks, programs, worries, illusions, challenges real and imagined. Clear to zero anything not serving my highest good and ultimate business abundance now."

CW: "My abundance flow is now strong. The universe sees my genius, wisdom and intelligence. This is rewarded with a strong steady flow of cash and a steady stream of happily paying clients. My ideas and business both experience untold healing and growth from this day onwards."

CW: "Raise self-belief, confidence and trust in myself and my products. When I raise self-belief people see me in a new light and I gain more credibility in the eyes of others and myself."

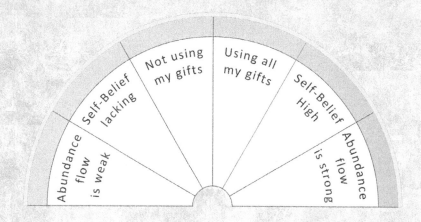

Not everything can be explained by science and nor should it have to. By keeping your mind open to wonder you are keeping the mystery and magic alive.

Transcending form begins with energy and memory. Finding new treasures will be easy today. Let go of linear thought and the universe will respond as you dream into being new timelines.

"I am so excited that my financial fate has now changed. I'm manifesting new opportunities for growth and change."

What % should I concentrate on one thing or many things?

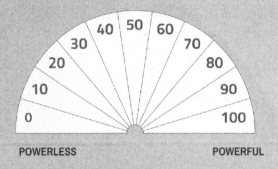

POWERLESS   POWERFUL

What % do I have a subconscious fear of scarcity?

"Clear fear of scarcity now to zero in all and every form from imprints to actual events. Completely clear to zero the charge in my solar plexus and root chakra, auric fields and energy and memory system. Clear fear of scarcity from brain stem, neural pathways and visual cortex system. Completely clear from my operating system now. Clear all hidden agendas resulting in fear and scarcity hidden in my neural networks now."

"I now activate and raise awareness of the flow and joy of universal abundance. I expect and trust that I will see it in my now timeline and lifetimes. I trust in the natural flow and expression of creative abundance which is all around me and flows through and to me."

"I now also balance giving and receiving. I am in balance. I know how to give as well as receive. It is my divine right to be able to fully receive abundance, health, wealth, love, joy and happiness. My heart is open to all these divine gifts and blessings now for my inner growth and well-being."

Being decisive

In a world where uncertainty rules, making decisive decisions and acting upon them might mean the difference between failure or success. Lucky that you have a pendulum and a pie chart to take the trauma out of decision making.

Pull all of your decisions into a pie chart and ask which option is best for you at this time.

"Enable me to be free of regrets
Enable me to easily take action
Enable me to be assertive and decisive
Raise subconscious awareness of my choices
Enable me to easily find the information I need
Enhance my ability to make
 decisions without fear
Increase confidence in ability to be pro-active."

What % is this decision going to help me?
What % am I good at making decisions?
What % of the time do I make decisions with no regrets?
What % of the time do I dwell of past mistakes?
What % of the time am I able to live with uncertainty?
What % of the time I do change my mind after making a decision?

Birthing creative flow

Call in Danu the goddess of creativity to activate these words.

"I open the portal of divine creativity and flow
I access the inner creative flow of all that is
I receive creative imagination, golden opportunities await for me to
birth the expression of light
I nourish myself and my creative timeline in this lifetime
Brain pathways activate for insights to flood my neural networks
I see creative vision with each and every step
Creativity is my birthright and I have the key to access its power
My ideas thoughts and dreams are anchored into this now reality
Allow inner expansive awareness of trust, truth and
creative energy to be my guiding light."

Blocks to inner magic

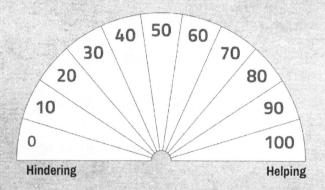

Hindering   **Helping**

Wanting things to happen too fast	_____
Not accessing power and magic of wisdom within	_____
Not believing in impossible dreams	_____
Not clearing past of all dramas	_____
Not being a friend to the self	_____
Not strengthening internal magic	_____
Not clarifying what you want to achieve	_____
Not knowing purpose of mission	_____
Not giving self permission to dream big	_____
Not clearing inner drama blocking view of self	_____
Thinking that you are not important	_____
Not trusting the vision your soul has for you	_____
Not connecting to higher self or source	_____
Having doubts about your ability to do things	_____
Not taking small steps each day	_____

Business Mindset

My business mindset is ...?
What % am I likely to achieve
_____ today?

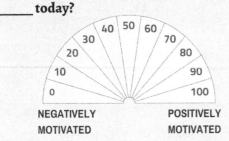

| NEGATIVELY | POSITIVELY |
| MOTIVATED | MOTIVATED |

CCW:

Let go of fear of completion around inaction
Reduce fear of deadlines and
fear of finishing projects
Decrease all financial burdens to zero

CW:

Enable me to dramatically increase my earning ability.
Increase positive motivation around my business.
Business angel find me the most loving clients.
Shift my negative energetic perspective around _____.
I let my business diversify and grow with love, fun and ease.
Let me be ordered, structured and powerful in my business.
I am in tune with my Soul purpose and mission.
Transform me into someone who is moving in the right inspired direction.
I believe in myself and my path is now known and shown.
Bring the right course/people/clients to me now with love and grace.
Install creative breakthroughs in my daily business energy.
Activate my inner business genius.
All my hard work is now paying off.

Change
your past

You can ask to energetically transform or change the energetic frequency in your past in this life or a previous life experience. Use the pendulum counterclockwise and ask it to 'find an event in the past that needs changing or transforming.'

Counterclockwise: "Find, locate and correct any situation or event in the past and then clear it or replace it."

Clockwise: " I now connect with a new higher vibrational version of myself in the past that _____."

When you choose to transform your past you also transform the present and the future timelines. You can dowse the truth of this statement.

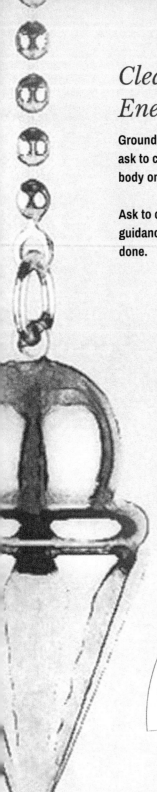

Clearing Non-Beneficial Energy

Ground, center and balance your energy -
ask to come back fully into the body. Test you are fully in your body on a zero to 100% chart.

Ask to connect to your higher self or source only for answers and guidance with zero other astral interference, check this has been done.

Ask to clear all non-beneficial energy from your healing space, pendulum, timeline and lifetime affecting this dowsing session.

Ask to bless the space with the highest frequency of love. Check this has been done.

Affirm your words are only to be used for highest healing and clearing and not a portal of energy that activates its conscious awareness.

Test the NBE has gone using this chart.

KEEP CLEARING NOT FULLY CLEARED

INTERFERENCE AFFECING DOWSING

FREE OF INTERFERENCE SAFE TO DOWSE NOW

Core limiting beliefs
around money/business

Check the % on any level in your now this timeline and reality you have any of these core limiting money beliefs around business or wealth.

You can clear them in one go using a counterclockwise pendulum spin.

- I need to conform
- I'll never have enough
- I'll never earn enough
- I can't get what I want
- Save for a rainy day
- There is never enough
- There is never enough time
- I'm blocked around money
- Others make more money easily
- Spiritual people are poor
- It's not right to want a lot
- Having is taking from others
- Rich people are dishonest
- I have to work all hours
- If you don't work hard you are lazy
- Money doesn't grow on trees
- I need to want to start a business

- I'm not good enough
- Life is hard
- No one sees me
- I'll never be successful
- Everything is expensive
- I can't afford marketing
- Cost of living is so high
- Why are they doing that
- That is my idea
- They stole that from me
- I wanted to do that
- Business is too stressful
- There is too much competition
- Marketing is too hard
- I give out so much and get nothing back

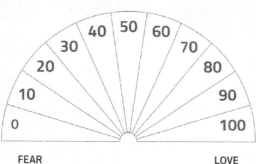

Creative Expression

Are you accessing your full creative flow and expression? Were you ignored as a child, not loved for the things you created from your heart? This can leave deep scars that remain hidden and only show themselves as not willing to try new things or for fear of rejection and disappointment.

If you are carrying fearful baggage give yourself permission to release that now which will enable you to harness inner creative energy and become a conscious creator of the universe. We can open dimensions to other doorways with our minds, thoughts, ideas and creations.

"I now give myself complete freedom to create with wonder, joy and freedom. Whatever happened in my past relating to creative expression has dissolved and resolved in my awareness and the fullness of time. I am grateful for these lessons. I am free to be me now."

Cycles of Time

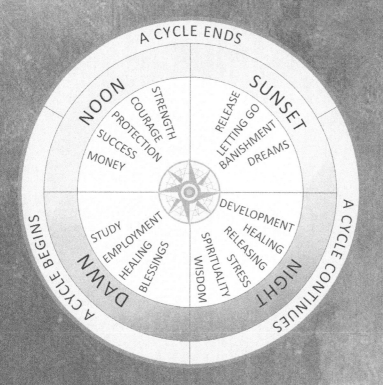

When we make a choice we create
an energetic shift point in time.
A cycle of time can begin or be ending.
Each cycle begins with a seed point,
a moment in time that creates a
pattern of events to follow.
This can be negative or positive.
Times of the day hold great potential
and power to change the past.

Ask to unlock a template of change which will unlock secrets to
activating successful choices in your life.

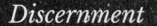

Discernment

How authentic is this message/person/situation?
How transparent and open?
What % is this false news designed to mislead?
In alignment with my higher truth?
How authentic is this channelled message?
Service to self or service to others?
Empowering or disempowering?
Harmful or harmonic?
Energetically strengthening or weakening?

Dew symbolises an inner transformation.
A vast consciousness is hidden within one drop of water.
The mystical and magical ability of water to transform, encode
and transmit is a powerful healing and universal life force.

The universe is speaking to you now and the conditions are
right for an alchemical transformation.
Combining dew in your energy healing work will bring you into
alignment with the gift of power with focus.

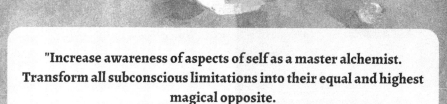

"Increase awareness of aspects of self as a master alchemist.
Transform all subconscious limitations into their equal and highest
magical opposite.

Correct all energetic mismatches between that which I want and
that which I believe I can receive. Cancel, clear and delete any
energetic blocks halting delivery and alignment with ease."

Emotional blocks
around money

Check if you are hiding any emotional blocks relating to the energy of money. Ask, "Around the issue of money what % am I experiencing any struggle?"

Struggle/Stress:

Likely the need to control events in your life is affecting your ability to connect with and receive info from your higher self.

Tired:

Ask to disconnect from overwhelm, exhaustion, drained and replace with energised, renewed, rested and strengthened.

Acceptance:

Look at areas such as self-esteem, limiting core beliefs and self-worth.

Unsupported:

Look at generational patterns within family lines of being unsupported and disconnect from them if necessary.

Repressed emotions:

Ask to connect to and clear any repressed emotional energy blocking financial flow. Increase personal financial integrity and strength.

Avoiding light:

What % can you see your inner brilliance? If it is low, raise it up higher.

Fear & Abundance

Fear shuts down divine flow and impedes transformation so dowse and check to see how much fear you are holding onto in relation to _____ for any particular issue or situation and check how much you are able to embrace change.

"Enable me to have the energy and strength in relation to leave behind outworn patterns or perspectives that no longer suit my highest good."

Use a clockwise command to install some positive energy around creating your own reality:

"I easily listen to my inner wisdom and access the realm of ideas, creativity, insights, magic, alchemy and divine flow now and always."

"I easily access passion and creative magic with inner freedom which represents my ability to be myself at a deeper level of alchemical transformation."

What % am I passionate about life?
What % do I have boundaries?
What % do I possess strength?
What % do I possess determination?
What % am I able to take consistent action?
What % am I focused?
What % am I driven?
What % am I free to create magic?
What % am I embarking on an alchemical transformation?

Freedom from overwhelm

Overwhelm is cleared now.
Enable me to experience a new
freedom from racing thoughts.
Allow me to experience divine timing.
I activate peace, calm and serenity now.
I release all programs of striving & surviving.
I love myself and easily focus on my needs.
I have all the time I need to achieve my dreams.
Time is an illusion and I transcend 3D boundaries.
Enable me to focus on one task at a time with ease.
I easily accept change is a natural process of life.
I live each day in the moment of love and freedom.
I allow myself to take time for myself with love.
I integrate & process information with ease.
Enable me to know I can operate freely
outside the boundaries of time & space.

Fun

*Sometimes in life we simply forget to have fun and enjoy the little moments.
When we raise our vibration, change perspective and seek out fun our life
changes for the better automatically.*

Enable me to see and switch
on the fun side of life again.
Enable me to make time for fun and
find others who resonate with this.
I now relax, let go of stress and
I am free to be myself again.
My focus is now on fun, expansion and joy.
I level up my ability to have fun.
I know how to have fun in my day to day life.
Fun knows where I am and
finds me even if I am hiding.
I see that life is a celebration and
I celebrate my time here.
I shift to the timeline of joy and peace.
I connect to the universal energy of fun
and freedom now.

What % am I blocked around fun?
What % do I make life fun?
What % do I allow fun and joy into my life?
What % am I inwardly resentul?

Goal setting

What % are you taking internal action?
What % do you need to take physical action?
What % do you have internal clarity on your vision?
How long do you need to visualise the outcome for?
How long do you need to journal for?
What % do you believe this is easy to achieve?
What % is this goal relevant for now?
What % is this goal soul aligned?
What % is this goal challenging enough?
Will this goal create life changes?
Is this goal detailed enough?

Use your pendulum and ask to remove all conscious and subconscious, internal and external limitations, blocks and obstacles to achieving these goals and dreams within a certain time frame.

Ask to remove all fear, worry and stress from these goals and that they are easily achievable within your now timeline.

Ask to remove inertia, procrastination and doubt. Connect to and clear to zero everything holding me back from taking the next step forwards.

"I am aware of what I need to do and how it needs to be done. This is easy for me now. I am relaxed about my path and in control of my destiny and growth."

JOY

CCW:

Clear to zero anger, overwhelm
and anxious like responses to life events.
Disconnect from self-sabotage, resentment and toxic energy.
Clear to zero all stress hormones and chemicals in the brain.

CW:

Connect to and restore ability to feel joy, peace and wonder.
Raise dopamine, oxytocin, serotonin to access more joy.
Enhance neurotransmitter functionality to experience joy.
Restore functionality of basal ganglia.
Activate orbitofrontal cortex for increased happiness.
Enable my new positive focus to see new openings and
opportunities.
My positive radiance opens new previously closed doorways.
Heal all doom and gloom in my timeline from point of creation.
I am blessed and feel safe to explore joy.

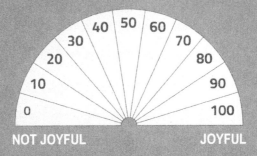

Dowsing pairs of words is a great exercise in how you are subconsciously feeling around any idea or part of your life. An example would be saying, "regarding my ability to manifest I am now _____".

I am now **Dowsing** *exercise*

This gives you real power to transform what might be blocking you at the subconscious level.

Suspicious	0 10 20 30 40 50 60 70 80 90 100	Trusting
Doubtful	0 10 20 30 40 50 60 70 80 90 100	Believing
Hateful	0 10 20 30 40 50 60 70 80 90 100	Loving
Resentful	0 10 20 30 40 50 60 70 80 90 100	Forgiving
Intolerant	0 10 20 30 40 50 60 70 80 90 100	Tolerant
Impatient	0 10 20 30 40 50 60 70 80 90 100	Patient
Lazy	0 10 20 30 40 50 60 70 80 90 100	Progressing
Angry	0 10 20 30 40 50 60 70 80 90 100	Calm
Fearful	0 10 20 30 40 50 60 70 80 90 100	Open
Envious	0 10 20 30 40 50 60 70 80 90 100	Grateful
Agitated	0 10 20 30 40 50 60 70 80 90 100	Peaceful
Frustrated	0 10 20 30 40 50 60 70 80 90 100	Successful
Limited	0 10 20 30 40 50 60 70 80 90 100	Boundless
Constricted	0 10 20 30 40 50 60 70 80 90 100	Expanded
Sad	0 20 30 30 40 50 60 70 80 90 100	Happy

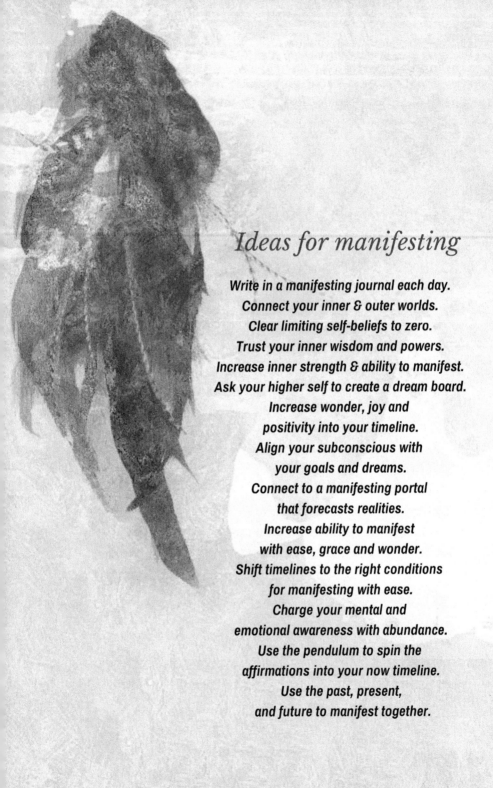

Ideas for manifesting

Write in a manifesting journal each day.
Connect your inner & outer worlds.
Clear limiting self-beliefs to zero.
Trust your inner wisdom and powers.
Increase inner strength & ability to manifest.
Ask your higher self to create a dream board.
Increase wonder, joy and
positivity into your timeline.
Align your subconscious with
your goals and dreams.
Connect to a manifesting portal
that forecasts realities.
Increase ability to manifest
with ease, grace and wonder.
Shift timelines to the right conditions
for manifesting with ease.
Charge your mental and
emotional awareness with abundance.
Use the pendulum to spin the
affirmations into your now timeline.
Use the past, present,
and future to manifest together.

I am the moon

Connect to the root cause of emotional instability and clear.
Clear to zero unresolved anxious thoughts and feelings.
Speak to the water in the body and send love.
Relax body, mind, and soul for my highest well-being.
Connect to the memory of fear and dissolve now.
Activate patience with myself and bring peace.

Clear to zero subconscious blocks to manifestation.
Affirm inner strength and ability to receive abundance.
Trust in my ability to create magic in my life with ease and grace.
Enable me to connect to the magic that is all around me easily.
Illuminate my path to self-care and healing.

Relax mind, body, and soul at a deep level of awareness.
Calm and balance the nervous system and promote rest.
Connect to my higher self for inner guidance and awareness.
Align with hidden wisdom and connect to my 'I AM' presence.

I am the sun

I AM THE SUN

I replenish, restore & repair.
I contain knowledge of advancement & wonder.
I allow you to begin anew.
I am the process of renewal, action & renovation.
I increase cellular awareness and restoration.
I speak through nature & creation with wisdom.
I help manifest the seemingly impossible & the improbable.
I contain codes, energy activation, symbols.
I help align you with the creative energy of the universe.
I activate personal alchemy, I strengthen positivity.
I increase inspiration to change and transform.
I help radiate inner belief & belief of inner power.

I AM THE SUN

Inner power

CCW:

Allow me to let go of people
and situations not
serving my highest good.

Clear to zero all 'other'
energy not mine.
Clear negative thought
forms in energy and memory.

Lift the burdens of others
affecting my auric field .
Release the 9 of Swords
from my energetic path.

CW:

I give myself permission
to feel love, joy and peace.
I am in command of my own
energy and power.
Increase creative self-expression.
I know I am whole now.
I know I am fearless now.
I know I am brilliant now.
I am standing in my own power.
My confidence, strength, wisdom and
energy have a high vibration.
I connect to the intelligence of
the universe for support.

Lightbody Energy

Our light body is an electromagnetic and sacred geometric grid of light that links our multi-dimensional self with the infinite universe. The light body transcends time and space and can help with ascension.

We can use the pendulum to assist with clearing, repairing and healing our light body to assimilate more light.

Ask to connect to your light body with the pendulum and then using a 0 - 100% chart test how connected you are to it before running the pendulum commands.

Counterclockwise:

"I clear cellular trauma and dark fearful duality programs
I clear all energy and memory of energy not of the light
I clear all light codes of pain, betrayal and fear
Decalcify my pineal for increased information and activation."

Clockwise:

"I program my solar plexus to be self-clearing, healing and strengthening
I raise my energy vibration and strengthen my light body auric fields
Increase the vibrational blessings of the food I eat
I give permission to strengthen my body with sacred geometry
I send healing and love to all parts of body, mind and soul
I awaken light codes and positive activations in my blood
I restore awareness as creator god/goddess divine
Increase vibrancy, charge and illumination from the Central Sun
I am a temple of light for light, radiating in light with light."

Limit on Success

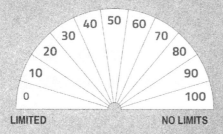

LIMITED   NO LIMITS

What % have I placed a limit on my own success?

CCW: " Clear all self imposed limitations and energy of lack residing in my thoughts, feelings, emotions, energy and memory system. I choose to connect to these imprints, tags, cords, words and imagery in non-local events and local events and reduce to zero in this and all other of my lifetimes."

CW: " I move beyond what is currently possible, from beyond the limited vision that I currently hold for myself. I rise upwards and shine. I give myself immediate permission to advance in all areas of my life from this point forwards."

"I am successful, rich and free
I am successful, rich and free
I am successful, rich and free"

Speed
Manifesting
Chart

My current manifesting speed is ?

Manifesting Wheel

Check using this dowsing wheel what is most powerful for you to do to bring in a manifestation or desired intention. First ask do I need something on this chart? YES/NO.

Mark each category out of 100% so you can discover what you need to do most to bring the manifestation in.

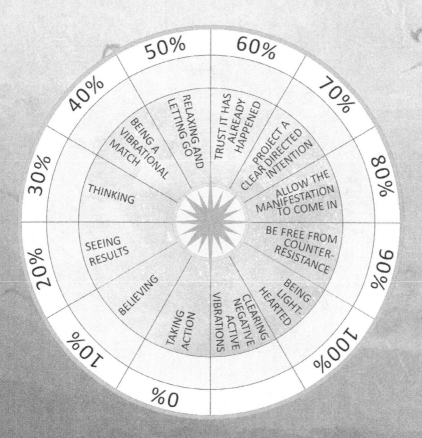

Mirrors

If the world is a mirror of our subconscious awareness then this command will enable you to download another person's consciousness and ability to do something you do not yet have the awareness of ....

"I now mirror your experience within my subconscious awareness."

Dowsing over a mirror will x the energy by 8 instead of doubling it. Dowse it to test this out.

Moon - New Beginnings
New Moon Ritual

Connect to and clear all energy of a
lower vibration not mine.
I revoke all non-beneficial energy and all
programs, cords, tags, ties and
conditioning from this and all dimensions.

I accept my path, surrender and move on
from everything holding me back.
I gracefully let go of all the struggle,
shame and fearful blocks keeping me small.
My current situation will now change for the better, I command it so
I am energy, youth and vitality, I see my own courage and strength
I am protected, powerful and wise.

I am always now guided by starlight so bright, so light .
New alchemical doorways of sacred
geometric awareness open wide.
I am a bridge between worlds,
my surroundings inspire my creative sight.
My intent and desire match my ability
to manifest and transform my life.

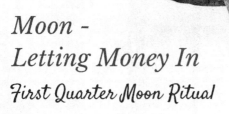

Moon - Letting Money In
First Quarter Moon Ritual

What % do I let money flow in?
What % do I believe I will become
financially free this lifetime?

I acknowledge a fresh start from within and
clear all negative perspectives. Around
money, I change the way I feel, think and act
around the energy of money.

My heart is open to giving and receiving money energy blessings.
Enable me to easily make decisions affecting my business.
I am ready to download a new consciousness awareness of wealth.
I clear doubts, fears, clouds, lack, loss, shame and self-blame.
I'm now excited to let money in.

Rigid inflexible paths of the past have now gone.
I expect to rise up, above limiting beliefs and fears of the past.
My light is on, money flows easily to me now.
I am blessed and worthy of riches.

I am comfortable receiving money.
I deserve to be paid for my energy, skills and expertise.
I feel my business is abundant.
Emotional resistance to money is gone.
I now receive money in new and unexpected ways.
I own my own value, I am amazing.

Moon - Cutting Cords
Third Quarter Moon Ritual

Where are you manifesting from? A place of lack or abundance?
Is your mindset rooted in joy, peace, happiness or fear?

I connect to and clear false
narratives & projections trapping wealth.
Clear all energetic control, fear &
unequal power from others over myself.
I now deactivate old energy tied up in
ancestral agreements diminishing power.

Connect to and clear to zero any past life, unresolved tensions,
mishaps, negative energy between
myself and person ____ affecting my business,
daily life or timeline now.

I connect to the biggest loss of
my inner power affecting my ability to
make money and receive money now
and clear that root cause to zero.

Harmonise all relationships in my
business, align with only the highest
images, holographic representations,
and intentions in everyday life.
I ask for a profound change to be activated in my now
timeline and swift positive developments
to affect my clients, business and reality.

Moon - Abundance
Full Moon Ritual

What % do I believe in my own mastery?
What % do I believe I can create
abundance in this life?

I am a powerful soul manifestor and creator of wealth.
Clear to zero any soul struggles relating to money creation.
Clear any hinderance or hidden aspects,
blocks, traps, fears & doubts.
Remove to zero hereditary/ancestral/
galactic/3D energy restrictions relating to
money energy and my belief in the ability to create wealth.

It is super easy for me to attract wealth
and draw it into the physical reality.

Silence the unwise voices from my mind, mine, and others
I free myself of old disappointments, confusion, and fear.
I now see opportunities where before were none.

I am now open, willing and commanding
abundance to be magnified in my life.
I energise and increase prosperity flow,
my ability to receive is increased.
Clear old beliefs around not being rewarded for work.
Re-align with ease, magnify opportunity, increase flow.
I know what to do, I am in flow.

Money belief blocks

Check if at any level in this reality you are carrying these belief blocks to being financially rich or affluent:

Resistance to being rich	0 10 20 30 40 50 60 70 80 90 100
Self doubt around ability	0 10 20 30 40 50 60 70 80 90 100
Fear of change	0 10 20 30 40 50 60 70 80 90 100
Fear of growth	0 10 20 30 40 50 60 70 80 90 100
Fear success	0 10 20 30 40 50 60 70 80 90 100
Fear rejection	0 10 20 30 40 50 60 70 80 90 100
Feeling stuck and unable	0 10 20 30 40 50 60 70 80 90 100
Feeling incapable	0 10 20 30 40 50 60 70 80 90 100
Feeling like in poverty	0 10 20 30 40 50 60 70 80 90 100
Feeling of scarcity	0 10 20 30 40 50 60 70 80 90 100
Fear high humbers	0 10 20 30 40 50 60 70 80 90 100
Feeling of standing still	0 10 20 30 40 50 60 70 80 90 100

Check if at any level in this reality these beliefs are blocking you from achieving wealth.

I must follow rules	0 10 20 30 40 50 60 70 80 90 100
My life will change	0 10 20 30 40 50 60 70 80 90 100
It's not safe to have freedom	0 10 20 30 40 50 60 70 80 90 100
It's not safe to be myself	0 10 20 30 40 50 60 70 80 90 100
I don't want life to change	0 10 20 30 40 50 60 70 80 90 100
It's easier to be poor	0 10 20 30 40 50 60 70 80 90 100
Success comes at a price	0 10 20 30 40 50 60 70 80 90 100
It's too much work	0 10 20 30 40 50 60 70 80 90 100
I don't have time	0 10 20 30 40 50 60 70 80 90 100
It's too much money	0 10 20 30 40 50 60 70 80 90 100
I can't do it alone	0 10 20 30 40 50 60 70 80 90 100

Money healing commands

CCW:

"All dis-empowering, negative stories woven into my inner 3D fabric, reality and now experience are unwoven, unlinked, dissolved and resolved.

All lack, loss, fear, anger, fright, frustration, grief and pain stored in my cellular carbon imagery as negative energy and memory are transformed.

Any and all of the above mirrored in the collective consciousness that exist within my neural networks are de-stressed and now blessed and sent to source for transmuting with love.

Clear, cancel and shift upwards to source any and all information, energetic patterns and beliefs stored in cellular energy and memory impeding my flow. I also cancel, remove and scramble all energetic imprints and implants holding me back from spiritual progression, evolution and inner wisdom. "

CW:

"I restore energetic flow, inner mastery and activate a deep inner knowing and understanding of my soul purpose and mission. This is revealed to me in a way I can directly access it and understand it.

I call in the strong independent creative visionary aspect of me now that resides in power, with power and of power. A lighthouse of discovery has been switched on within. I am imprinted with the highest light codes of awareness, trust, peace, freedom and grace.

What was asleep for my highest good has now been awakened in memory and energy system to guide and enable to me realise mastery over matter. I evoke the power to manifest with light. "

Money healing commands

Clear resistance to and fear of growth and expansion
Clear doubt and fear of my own inner power
Clear fear of change and transformation
Clear fear of today, the past, and tomorrow
Clear fear of success, happiness and joy
Clear fear of high numbers
Clear fear of rejection, fear of being different

"Source remove all subconscious fears, blocks and challenges directly affecting my ability to create abundance, achieve inner growth and receive inspiration.

Source directly now remove all experiences of negativity from fear, drama, lack, loss. Clear to zero all known and unknown abundance blocks, traps, fears and beliefs hiding in the fabric of time and space affecting my timeline and energy now.

Banish distortions in the collective connected to indecision, procrastination and worry attached to the energy of money.
Disconnect from all soul junk obscuring my path now. "

CW:

"I give myself permission to allow self love and to set myself free at the subconscious level and weave a new empowering life story.

I am now able to program source for my best and highest timeline harming none.
This is easy for me now.

A stargate has opened within and above me that I can access at anytime. It is full of pure energetic magic and heart charged love and bliss. I now align with growth, prosperity and allow myself to be open to receive great blessings. I have opened a stargate, a cosmic portal to dream building, expansion and illumination."

My business

What % am I on the right track with this idea?
What % do I need to outsource?
What % am I able to start a business?
What % is this the right idea for me now?

I am proud of my ideas and achievements in business.
Creative ideas that sell well come to me easily.
I meet others who share my vision and we help each other.
Clients easily find and can afford me.
I set achievable goals and effortlessly reach them.
I have the energy, insight and clarity to start a new business.
I easily tap into new skills and bring through creative dreams.
Marketing and advertising effortlessly fall into place.
I'm so excited about my business ideas.
The power of my ideas are phenomenal.
Allow my innate skills, gifts and
talents to be easily recognised.
I am filled with hope, calm and
the ability to share my message.
I experience an explosion of
happiness and business success.
Enable me to learn easily from business challenges.
My business moves forwards in remarkable ways.
Crazy amazing opportunities are
happening for me right now.

New moon Beliefs

Test your beliefs using a percentage chart and install new beliefs at a subconscious level. This is easy to do and works dramatically at a deeper level to assist with manifesting.

- Manifesting is easy for me   0 10 20 30 40 50 60 70 80 90 100
- I know I can achieve success   0 10 20 30 40 50 60 70 80 90 100
- I have everything I need   0 10 20 30 40 50 60 70 80 90 100
- The world wants me to succeed   0 10 20 30 40 50 60 70 80 90 100
- The universe is supporting me   0 10 20 30 40 50 60 70 80 90 100
- Now in the right time to make changes   0 10 20 30 40 50 60 70 80 90 100
- I easily step out of my comfort zone   0 10 20 30 40 50 60 70 80 90 100

- I love trying new things   0 10 20 30 40 50 60 70 80 90 100
- I'm geared for success   0 10 20 30 40 50 60 70 80 90 100
- I love my life   0 10 20 30 40 50 60 70 80 90 100
- I am determined to achieve my desires   0 10 20 30 40 50 60 70 80 90 100
- I am emotionally stable   0 10 20 30 40 50 60 70 80 90 100
- Wishes do come true   0 10 20 30 40 50 60 70 80 90 100
- Money is easy to make   0 10 20 30 40 50 60 70 80 90 100
- My habits support my dreams   0 10 20 30 40 50 60 70 80 90 100
- The timing is right for me to excel   0 10 20 30 40 50 60 70 80 90 100

Any beliefs not congruent with your goals and dreams you can use the pendulum to shift the energy around them with a simple command:

CCW: "Clear all my unhelpful limiting beliefs and subconscious self-sabotage around 'Money is easy to make'.

CW: "Install and set the most positive highest vibration aligned with my inner wishes, hopes and dreams and call in the vibration of this energy down to earth."

Noticing magic

The act of noticing magic calls it into your now timeline and reality.

What % do you subconsciously believe you can create magic or influence your external reality?

What % is anything on this planet or any other planet blocking my ability to be incredibly wealthy?

Clockwise:

Magnify my ability to be wealthy.
Correct energetic wealth
patterns to positive.
Access hidden avenues of wealth.
Increase my ability to create wealth
magic. The result I want to see is
increased wealth now.
Activate a sympathetic
and parasympathetic
resonance to inner and outer wealth.
Great things are always happening.
I remember now how to be wealthy.
I remember how to work magically.
Increase and activate inner magical
resonance and belief.
Shift to a timeline of increased
magical awareness and activity.

Open to wisdom

Check the percentage you are open to receiving wisdom, new tools, knowledge and information.

CW:

"Raise my ability to be open to receiving new tools, knowledge, downloads and wisdom for my highest intelligence and well-being. Increase my creative intelligence to maximum. I see greater potential in the everyday energy all around me and access a deeper wisdom from the world around me.

I uncover more truths about the universe each day and the universe supports and guides me in my business. Ideas come to me out of the blue with spontaneous ease, grace and magical wonder.

I choose to be present and to participate fully in this earth life. It is safe for me to activate my unique powers, talents, gifts and abilities.

I believe in myself and have the power, strength and energy to achieve my goals and desires. I seek and easily connect to the right timeline for inner magic."

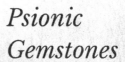

Psionic
Gemstones

All energy exists and can directed at will from within the astral.

Commanding the intelligence of the universe can be used to accomplish tasks.

Ask to be able to consciously direct energy and power with intent.

" I am now attuned to the magic and power of all psionic gemstones. I am able to consciously direct crystal arrows from my energy system with direct commands to bring me _____."

Repelling or creating wealth

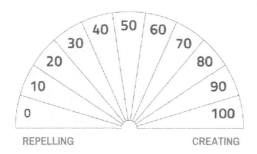

REPELLING   CREATING

All things in the universe considered what % am I repelling or creating wealth today?

CCW: "Connect to and erase limiting money paradigms and any limiting conditioning money program templates within.

Release struggle and hard work consciousness tied to creativity, achieving and receiving great wealth.

Cancel, clear and delete all programs running in the background containing fear, lack and scarcity from my energy and memory system now."

CW:

"Enable me to subconsciously
vibrate and equate wealth to awareness
with wonder. Wealth conscious creation
codes upgrade, switch on and activate within me.

My frequency attracts, generates and manifests
wealth easily like never before."

Perceived v Actual value

What is my perceived value compared to my actual value?

Empaths, lightworkers and healers are prone to giving everything away and not great at receiving. If we are to set up a stable, long-term business we need to own our value and stop giving everything away for free.

CW: "Enable me to believe in my own gifts, skills and abilities. I now take time to restore my inner power and value. I am able to correctly charge for my expertise and wealth of knowledge.

I choose to see myself in a new illuminating and powerful light. I am paid well for my gifts, my services and my talents.

I choose to feel at peace with charging the correct price to reflect my value."

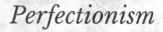

Perfectionism

Counterclockwise:

I clear the subconscious belief that
making a mistake is wrong.
I clear impossible standards that rule
my behaviour and work flow.
Cancel and clear inner critic and
all worry around disappointing others.
Clear belief I have to be and do my very
best at all times despite other pressures.
Clear to zero I have to work harder
than anyone else and be perfect.
Disconnect from my own high
standards and associated
subconscious beliefs.

Clockwise:

I know it is ok to make mistakes
Mistakes are part of learning and being creative
I know I cannot please everyone all the time
It is ok to be myself and go with the flow
Increase patience with self and the process
Increase ability to accept my own work
with all its beautiful flaws.

Self love

**What % do you listen
to the wisdom of
your heart?**

CCW:

*Remove to zero all blocks, limitations
and challenges to experiencing self-love.
Remove all emotional burdens and restore
a sense of peace, trust and wonder.*

CW:

*Activate self-love and a sense of inner trust and respect.
Enable the heart chakra to fully give and receive love.
The flower of energy around my heart is flowing with love.
Transform myself into someone who loves myself fully.
Imprint at the subconscious level it is ok to love again.
Restore emotional healing on all levels affecting physical reality.
Enable me to know that is it ok to
use my heart for powerful things.*

Self sabotage

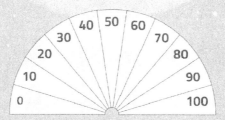

What % of negative subconscious self-sabotaging beliefs do I hold in my energy or memory system that are affecting my now timeline around business and productivity?

"I clear to zero all subconscious negative self-sabotaging beliefs, worries and fears affecting my confidence levels and ability to be visible in this world. Clear all fears and past triggers embedded in my subconscious affecting my ability to be responsible, self-sufficient and empowered."

"I affirm my right to be able to manifest my dream business with ease and grace. I am free from the past and new people, ideas and resources manifest easily into my now timeline. I see new opportunities that were previously hidden."

"My hidden blocks resulting from trauma are now working in my favour, they are a vast resource for others to learn and benefit from. Everyone sees my strength. All past blocks and limitations are now a gold mine of energetic potential, freedom and wisdom. Other people see my worth at a subconscious level and look to me for guidance and support. I affirm my worth each and every day, I am unstoppable."

Subconscious beliefs

What % do I have limiting subconscious beliefs around my capabilities or the abundance of money in the universe?

" Clear to zero and destabalise any and all limiting beliefs affecting my ability to create and maintain an amazing flourishing business for my highest good and healthiest bank account."

" I expect to be flooded with high paying clients who love my products and services and see my value and worth. I draft in new and helpful business guides who show me the way and help me succeed easily and fast. I fast track my now this life experience with wealth creation."

" I now re-wire all negative cellular beliefs and energy around money and abundance. I know that words are triggers of energetic situations which result in timeline changes and transformations. I clear to zero all positive-negative charges relating to words such as failure, not having and struggle. I replace the energy of these words with expectation of positive happenings and new support whenever one of these words is mentioned in my life."

The energy of time

"Time you are now on my side.
I have all the time I need.
My energy and vitality
increase with passing time.
All energy wounds caused
over time are now removed.
I now have time to restore, repair and replenish.

I work with harmony, resonance and time.
I activate advanced cellular repair and rejuvination.
I am now able to bend time and space.
The universe is benevolent.
It is safe for me to open up to higher
inner dimensions of time and space.

I align with the energetic frequency of time.
I access advanced time nodes now.
The energy of the future is
contained within my body.
I access advanced intelligence now.
I access time repair body mode healing now.
It is now my time to receive _____.
I increase the visibility of money
 in my now timeline.
Ask to jump timelines for
positive outcomes.
Ask to do healing outside the
boundaries of time and space."

Time v money

Dowse what do you need more of? Time or money?

Money is a renewable resource that you can always get back however you cannot so easily reclaim back time. This card instructs you that taking action cannot wait any longer. The sooner you take action the sooner you will see results. It is never too late to start something new.

If you believe you have wasted or lost money with a purchase that did not give you a good return for your money you can ask to retrieve lost funds. I did this twice and funds were returned sometimes within a day.

What % can I easily retrieve lost funds?

CW: "Enable me to retrieve back lost funds from _____."

The
Magic of
Rainwater

Rainwater has energetic properties that contain elements connected to weather so a storm will contain elements of fire.

Collect rainwater for drinking or water imprinting for extra power.

Use it for:

- *New beginnings, change and growth*
- *Releasing old patterns and negative energy cycles*
- *Clearing distorted lines of energy flow*
- *Focusing, manifesting and becoming inspired*
- *Increasing imagination and inner wisdom*
- *Attunes you to nature so you vibrate higher*
- *Increases flow with time and space*
- *Removes exhaustion and mental confusion*
- *Increases strength and links past, present and future*
- *Breathes life into new projects with mystical mastery*
- *Increases cellular communication at the vibrational level*

The
Power of Water

Water is living information and
can be structured and programmed to
facilitate communication between the
cells and tissues of the body for vitality.

Any vibration can be imprinted into the
consciousness of water. You can use
colour, sound, numbers, words, pictures,
or any vibrational frequency.

The energy of water is more powerful
than its material substance.

Water absorbs information and
transmits that information where it
goes to. Thoughts are absorbed by water.

Water can read information from words.

Water can be blessed, purified, cleansed,
asked to bring healing. Water is a living
and intelligent consciousness.

Use a pendulum clockwise to imprint the
energetic vibration of something positive
into your drinking water like a word such
as peace or harmony.

Expand and increase my awareness of what is possible

Increase intelligence of light fields and forces beneficial

Level up to another dimension of awareness and perception

Access inner library of ancient mystical and magical knowledge

I am a powerful force of manifesting light

I tap into creative wisdom from intelligent light sources

Attune my frequency to manifest even faster

Decipher hidden energy and memory codes

Access information from the future and reclaim understanding

As I think it, it is done now

Re-map brain pathways to see more metaphysics

The invisible is the new visible

I am shown my mission, this is clear as day

Restore metaphysical sight to full capacity

I fully understand, accept and believe in my inner power

I am now fully aware, awake and understand energy

Increase my natural ability to be peaceful and powerful

Change trajectory and timeline to see, renew and become anew

Access a new understanding of an old situation or event

*Which symbol, colour, shape, sound or picture represents me at
the 12th Dimension?*

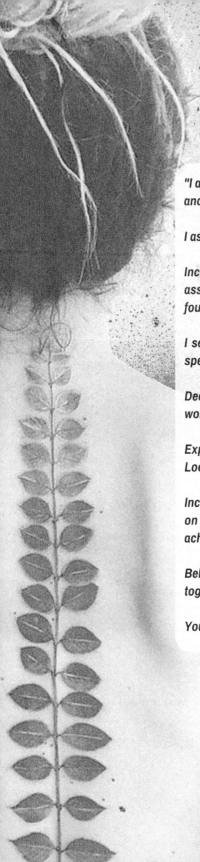

The spirit of money
channelled message

"I am the spirit of money, I connect and direct, change and transform. I am a force and an agent of change.

I ask you to demand and command me.

Increase my creative flow in your life. Call on me for assistance with vibration, abundance, flow, foundation, support, freedom and empowerment.

I set plans into action. Increase deserving and joy of spending within your subconscious programming.

Decrease pride, mistrust, fear, envy, sabotage and worry.

Expand your thinking and try new things.
Look at the % you choose comfort over progress.

Increase ability to do more in less time. Find and stay on the path of success. Raise expectation of achievements, opportunity and lucky breaks.

Believe in me, I am on your side. We will work together in new and beautiful ways.

You are blessed now."

The world is a magical place

How you view the world and your place in it will
directly affect your ability to manifest.
Are you manifesting from a space of wonder and magic or
fear and resentment?

*"I ground, anchor and center my ability to create money. I now
connect my ability to earn money with freedom, ease,
grace, harmony and love at the subconscious level of creation.*

*All fears, disappointments, resentments, lack, loss and
subconscious negative patterns are cleared to zero now.*

*I am now ready, willing and able to
shift my relationship to money.
Money is easy for me to come by, readily available.*

*The universe is waiting to give me gifts.
I am ready, I am aware, I am focused.
Everything changes for me now.
Money is energy and I am that energy.*

*I see a new fundamental shift as I
re-imagine my future. I imprint inner power and embody the
expression of what is now possible within my energy
and memory. I am a creative power like no other."*

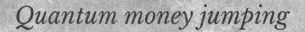

Quantum money jumping

I instantly release all troubling blocks
around money in my now timeline
Ask that energetic solutions are
instantly found on your new timeline
Ask to be in quantum alignment
with the amount of your choice
On this new timeline all limiting
beliefs are erased as if by magic
I love the energy of money and it
is now visible within my timeline
I am feeling a magnetic shift towards
the energetic attraction to wealth
Money as an energy is so easy to attract
Money is sent directly to me to use how I please
I have manifested $100,000 and see it in
my now timeline and this lifetime

$100,000

Universe as a hologram

Some theories teach that the universe is holographic and that we can access and change the holographic template to one that suits us more.

It is thought that our bodies are also holographic and that our cells contain all the information about all our other cells.

If everything in the universe is intelligent information we can access this information just by requesting to.

The author has downloaded genius and graphic design creativity just by asking to and spinning the pendulum clockwise.

We can direct etheric crystalline energy to parts of the energetic body, jump timelines and magnetically draw vibrational frequencies or experiences into our timeline for our highest good and well-being.

"Connect to my own highest and best magical timeline. I am elevated with enchantment and wonder and hold the key to all the elements I need for creative expansion. I am free to be myself and experience the expression of creativity, love and freedom."

Validation

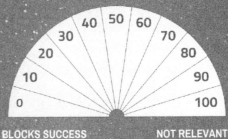

BLOCKS SUCCESS   NOT RELEVANT

How much does being invalidated in childhood still block your success today?

CCW: "Clear to zero all invalidation blocks, trauma and challenges from childhood causing negative feelings, images, low self-worth, self-esteem and lack of confidence. "

"Remove all triggers and negative reactions from the time of childhood affecting my ability to connect to and be happy with who I am. Clear all responses from adults, carers, teachers and parents resulting in shame, pain and blame. Clear to zero any and all trapping energy limiting my ability to be brilliant in this now lifetime."

"I disentangle and disengage from all family trauma and dramas of the past. All past and fearful events are now null and void."

CW: I am now free and able to make choices based on certainty, trust, freedom and passion."

Your Beliefs Shape Matter

Do you hold any
limiting beliefs
about the universe?

Is it possible to raise
consciousness by asking to?

Is the universe made of
frequencies of light?

Do you
subconsciously align with
your goals and dreams?

Are your beliefs mostly
positive or negative?

We are all made of light
in the creative force of nature
We can easily change timelines
We are all connected
Our body responds to our thoughts
The universe hears our thoughts and responds
We can leave ourselves gifts on our timeline
Each day can bring new wisdom
Clearing blocks is fun and easy
We can turn genes on or off
We can change the energy of the past
Energy is accessed through picture, word and intention.
The pendulum is a tool for self-development using light

Your current money story

Limiting
Low vibrational
money story

Empowering
High vibrational
money story

You can check to see if you are carrying a low vibrational energetic money story around with you.
This will be limiting beliefs around how much you can earn or manifest either based on your world view or maybe parental conditioning.

What % are you holding onto a low vibration money story?
What % is this limiting your ability to manifest?
What % is this disempowering yourself at any level?
What % are you using this as an excuse not to take action?
What % are you ready for change?

Ask to reconnect to any hidden energy behind those fears or limiting money stories and to gain inner freedom and new money energy wisdom.

The power of symbols

It is said that the universe speaks to us in signs and symbols.

Symbols are archetypes of energy, power, and vibration that hold deep meaning, illumination and hidden inner wisdom. They also have the power to awaken universal consciousness within us for expansion and growth. They are familiar to us and so very powerful.

Our subconscious mind operates using the power of symbolic language and can be easily accessed using art imagery and symbolism.

Tribal medicine utilises symbolism for body and energy healing and transformation.

You can access the source of divine power directly with the use of symbols. They are one of the easiest ways to connect with the universal energy that surrounds us for manifesting, clearing or healing.

Gazing at a symbol acts as a trigger that expands perception,and awakens consciousness, growth, ascension and inner power.

When you use magical symbols you are magnifying your own inner power and strength by raising your frequency and opening portals and doorways that will access more information and knowledge.

Find a symbol you are drawn to and research its meaning or give it meaning that resonates with you. You can imprint the energy of any frequency in the universe into a symbol and use it as a talisman.

Connect with a symbol using the pendulum and spin the energetic power into your timeline or into a situation that needs healing or repairing.

Draw a symbol on the body or on a piece of paper and put it on the body for healing or wisdom.

A protection symbol such as the Awe of Helm can be placed in the home or on a sacred geometric grid with the intention to protect and keep you safe from harm.

A symbol can be a catalyst for healing deep trauma and clearing old wounds that reside in the collective conscious memory and energy. Put your hand on the symbol and ask to integrate any repressed shadow energy blocking your ability to move forward.

Baglamukhi Yantra
Protection with prosperity stability

Protection from enemies with prosperity and stability
Protection against diseases, chronic problems, and accidents
Success in legal matters and improves any financial situation
Removes negative energy in your surroundings
Removes curses, vows, and negative energy sent to destroy you
Helps with illumination on the journey and life path
Releases heavy responsibility in life weighing you down

Bee Energy
Symbol of divine feminine

*The bee represents creativity, imagination and divine inspiration.
Also a symbol for wisdom, focus and self-generation.*

*Call upon the spirit of the bee for fast action, to manage your personal
energy flow and help focus time, energy and effort.*

The Bee is the Master Builder.

*"Believe in your inner magic and power, small steps
can move mountains if you trust yourself and your place
within the universe."*

Dragonfly
Symbol of inner freedom

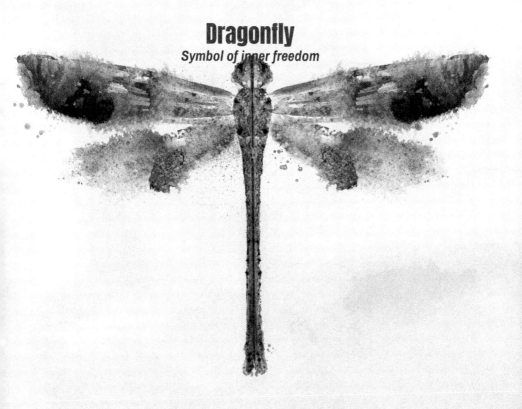

*If you are called to work with the energy of the dragonfly you
can be sure that some part of you is breaking free of the past.*

*New insights and energy are likely to come in fast as a final clearing
takes place entwined with magic. The dance of the dragonfly
brings a liberation and clearing of repeated energetic patterns
that were holding you back or keeping you trapped.*

CCW over this image to finally free yourself from past limitations

*CW: to call upon breakthrough magic that raises your energy and
vibration fast.*

Energy Sphere
Completion & Divination

Protection
Spheres are excellent for protection.
Place yourself into an energy sphere of
your own design, material & frequency.

Sphere of Unlimited Potential

See your future self living the life you desire.
See the now you version of yourself merging with your future self.
Place yourselves into the sphere and the sphere into your solar plexus.
Your future self is communicating with your this life self.
For manifesting situations and opportunities to co-engineer a new reality.

Eye of Kanaloa
Total Confidence

Represents the web of life and
the 8 consciousness realms.
The harmony of love and power.
The star represents the Higher Self.
The rings represent Earth, Air, Fire and Water.

Use this for Physical Etheric Energy healing
or for Manifestation by spinning the pendulum
over the grid to activate the energy within you
whilst stating your intention.

You can also put your hand over it to activate

Eye of Ra
Protection - Connection - Magic

Use as a protective shield or amulet.
Dissolves psychic attacks.
Activates intuition, healing and third eye insight.
Good for magical altar work.

Kali Yantra
The Goddess of Fire & Change

A transformer for healing and symbolises the Mother of Time
Enhances the power of action and acts as an agent of internal force
As a geometric symbol, the yantra represents everything that can be
internalised in our conscious awareness
Gaze at the symbol or activate the force of Kali within your timeline
I am power and have power, I am rebirth and a new dawn
I regenerate matter, I am the consciousness of matter
I remove all fear and increase inner power

Levels of consciousness
Conscious - Subconscious - Superconscious

Conscious
Represents the daily mind and thought processes.

Subconscious
Lower brain and spine - Connect to your subconscious
for faster manifesting.

Superconscious
The realm of true creativity, genius, knowledge & insight.

Metatron's Cube

Metatron - The Archangel of Manifesting

Purification - Manifestation - Transformation - Grounding - Protecting

*I connect with the building blocks of all consciousness, energy, and matter
All forms of intelligence and life are contained within this
structure and are also within you
Place your focused intention in the centre of the
cube and place this within your heart.*

Also use as a charging station for crystals, essences, and water imprinting.

Sri Yantra

meaning "Instrument of power"

This 12,000-year-old symbol is thought to be the key to obtaining all earthly desires and material manifestation. Will connect you to universal consciousness and can open pineal gland.

Gaze at the symbol and focus on that which you wish to manifest. The symbol is a portal for unlocking greater intelligence.

The 7 Spiral Chart

Use this chart to dowse which area of self-empowerment the energetic frequency contained within the spiral can help you with. The spiral is a living vortex of powerful energy and can help transmute resistance and clear blocks.

It is a powerful energy tool to utilise for reaching your highest potential, realising your creativity and having energetic breakthroughs.

The 7 spirals represent a different area of empowerment. Dowse to see where you need energetic releasing or energising.

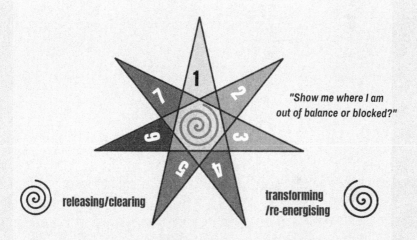

"Show me where I am out of balance or blocked?"

releasing/clearing

transforming /re-energising

Key "Restore the energy needed around 1-7 for my highest health and well-being."

1. Deserving	Release the frequency of shame and increase self-worth
2. Creating	Release fear of being visible and increase proactivity
3. Power	Release anger and increase self-confidence
4. Openess	Release old wounds and increase self-love
5. Expression	Release low self-esteem and increase expansion
6. Vision	Release limiting world views and increase clarity
7. Purpose	Release limited self thoughts and increase inner purpose

The 12 universal laws
of financial prosperity

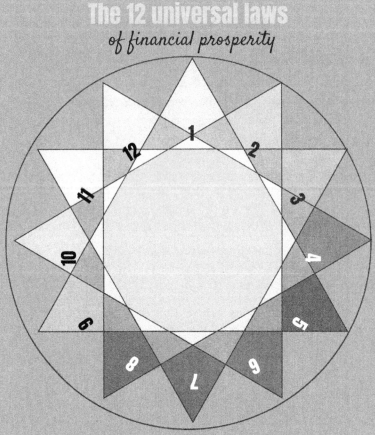

12 represents the symbolic creation of the universe

1. *The law of abundance - shift your beliefs*
2. *The law of attention - focus on the positive*
3. *The law of attraction - shift your thoughts*
4. *The law of clarity - making a clear decision*
5. *The law of flow - let go of blocks*
6. *The law of giving and receiving - balance this*
7. *The law of intention - be specific*
8. *The law of manifestation - drawing energy in*
9. *The law of non-attachment - let go of end result*
10. *The law of prosperity - honour your gifts*
11. *The law of success - achieving goal mastery*
12. *The law of positivity - raise emotional vibrancy*

Dowse to see which law you most need to pay atttention to for financial growth

The Ankh
Ancient Egyptian symbol - The Key of Life

Protection - Wisdom - Regeneration - Power

I fully tune into my inner heart - mind - soul aspects.
I open portals of magic and mystery for divine abundance.
Increase intuitive wisdom with creative perception.
Access the codes and keys of hidden divine knowledge.
Clear, cancel, and delete the hold of others taking my power.
Restore my life strength in my timeline now.
Anchor in the cellular energetic commands needed
for restoration, health, and wealth.

The Energy Spiral

The spiral is fundamental to nature and a symbol for profound creation and growth. Spiral art can be seen in ancient civilisations dating back to 3200 BC. The spiral represents the consciousness of nature, form and evolutionary development.

Within energy healing a counterclockwise spiral represents clearing, releasing and banishing unwanted energy. The clockwise spiral represents balance, progress, expansion, awareness, connection, strength and journeying.

Spirals can reset or energise the energy flow within the human body and auric fields and release blocks to divine creative expression. A spiral can also be used to slow down or speed up time.

Spin a spiral into your timeline,business or creative project.

Place a spiral on the body for energy or healing.

Energise water with a spiral under the glass of water.Dowse to see if you need a counterclockwise or clockwise energy spiral for healing.

The Mountain
Symbol of strength, energy, and power

Balances yin & yang
Activates ability to stand in own power
Signifies mastery over matter
Realising own power and potential
Connects to the present time

"In this situation I am strong, and
I know how to take inspired action."

The Philospher's Stone
Manifesting the impossible

It is now possible for me to manifest the impossible.

My time, energy and attention are
aligned with universal flow.
New intelligence awakens within.
I create matter outside of time and space.

The Platonic Solids
Sacred Geometry & the building blocks of creation

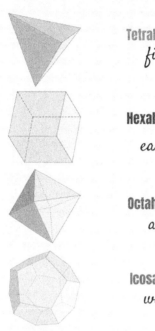

Tetrahedron

fire

Access the power
of the mental body, use
for mind expansion & focus

Hexahedron

earth

Slows down the physical energy
and matter. Use for manifesting
and grounding etheric into
consciousness of earth

Octahedron

air

Use for self-awareness & finding
opportunities. The consciousness of
air activates hidden wisdom and
inner knowledge

Icosahedron

water

Symbols for replenishing,
magical and will connect to and
clear all things that have gone wrong
within your lifetime

Dodecahedron

ether

Experiences the multi-dimensional
reality of the universe and contains
manifesting power from within
the etheric realm

Visualise the platonic solids to connect to
the consciousness & energetic flow represented by these symbols.
All wisdom and knowledge of reality can be accessed through these shapes.
They can open or close time portals within your energy and memory system.
Open a dialogue with them and see what wisdom comes through

The Rose Compass
Finding your North Star - Dowsing Chart

When you find your North Star you know where you are headed.
You can use the North of the compass to follow your North Star.
Say, "As I connect to my inner compass, what direction am I
heading in regarding the situation of _____."
You can make up other dowsing answers for the other compass
points. Below are correspondences relating to the compass map.

North	South	East	West
Infinite	Now	Future	Reflection
Potential	Fire	New	Focus
Home/Wisdom	Passion	Beginnings	Confidence
Creativity	Creation	Trust	Business
Security	Strength	Compassion	Energy
Adaptability	Adventure	Communication	Movement

The Triquetra
The power of 3

Mind ~ Body ~ Spirit
Past ~ Present ~ Future
Life ~ Death ~ Rebirth
Thoughts ~ Feelings ~ Action
Ego ~ Self ~ Shadow

Using this symbol for manifesting by:

Holding the mental thought in your mind.
Combine that thought with emotion from heart.
Pull this energy/vision down into your earth star chakra,
also known as the millionaire chakra.

Bless the energy and space you just created.

Triangle symbol

Use for raising vibration & focused
manifestation

Symbolises matter, focus, and conscious creation
Represents knowing, feeling & action
Also time, space, and energy

Focus on this picture and ask it to remove any negative
wealth imprints that do not serve your highest good
Blink and then ask to replace with the energetic vibration
of magical creation or anything you desire to manifest

This picture will also amplify anything into your life you place
upon it as well as your energetic vibration

Find the author

My etsy shop carries a range of divination tools for energy healing. My second book can be purchased as a spiral book and comes with a teaching license so you are free to use it to teach others how to use the pendulum.

This book is also available as a colour spiral from etsy.

https://www.etsy.com/uk/shop/TheDivinationPath

Teaching

You can find my online course with reviews here that covers using the pendulum for dowsing and healing in depth. 50% off offer exists as you have bought this book - use the coupon 'ibelieve' at checkout.

https://thedivinationpath.thinkific.com/courses/the-pendulum-healing-course

"You're amazing... you will be on the international circuit speaking one of these days - your work is incredible."

Download the full set

"She will create the tools for people's transformation"

Ebook PDF Bundle - 10 divination and dowsing pendulum healing books which is about 800 pages of dowsing and healing magic with charts, commands and pendulum ideas for energy healing, manifesting and self empowerment.

Follow me

New dowsing books and decks are being produced all the time. Follow my work and teachings in my facebook group 'The Art of Manifesting' here:

https://www.facebook.com/groups/theartofmanifesting

Printed in Great Britain
by Amazon